TABLE OF CONTENTS

INTRODUCTION: A STRATEGY IN NAME ONLY

The 2012 policy update to the National Defense Strategy, "Sustaining U.S. Global Leadership: Priorities for the 21st Century," makes a very bold strategic statement: "we will out of necessity rebalance toward the Asia-Pacific region."[1] This policy update is intended as a roadmap for the next ten years; what is not completely clear in this document is why there is a strategic need to rebalance. There is also no indication as to how the United States intends to accomplish this rebalance, what it will require, or how long it will take. The validity and logic of this strategy will be examined using a foundationally sound Ends, Ways, and Means model. The result of this examination is an assessment that the U.S. strategy pronouncement is flawed, as it does not address the right questions, and ultimately uses budget constraints to determine a strategy. This flawed approach creates the rationale for potential military escalation that is unnecessary and could lead to a confrontation in a time and place contrary to U.S. interests. Because this flawed strategy could weaken the United States as the dominant world power, a complete reassessment is necessary.

THE U.S. STRATEGIC POSITION IN ASIA: 1945 AND 2012

In many ways the strategic situation facing the United States in 2012 resembles conditions in the Asia-Pacific region immediately after World War II. As in 1945, the United States in 2012 is addressing an economic imbalance resulting from wartime expenditures and excessive deficit spending. As in 1945, the administration is taking

---

[1] President Barack Obama, *Sustaining U.S. Global Leadership: Priorities for the 21st Century Defense*, (Washington DC: Government Printing Office), 2012, 2.

1

steps to reduce spending by cutting the defense budget. And as was the case in 1945, there is the consideration of a threat from a major power perceived to be seeking to dominate the region.

Although an exact parallel between the 1945 and 2012 cannot be drawn, these three significant factors highlighted above illustrate the need for a comprehensive strategic approach. This comprehensive approach is called a grand strategy. Grand strategy in practice "is the theory, or logic that binds a country's highest interests to its daily interactions with the world."[2] The concepts as well as definitions of strategy have been debated by many scholars and strategy theorists. For example, Williamson Murray and Mark Grimsley remarked that "strategy has proven notoriously difficult to define."[3] It has also eluded Sir Michael Howard who determined he "could find no definition of it."[4] While there are many variants of the definition of grand strategy, there are common attributes found within various definitions.[5] The following commonality emerges: a framework or process of determining desired ends, based on enduring values or long term interests, then applying the nation's resources through the nation's instruments of power. While developing a grand strategy is a complex undertaking, America has proven in the past a capability to do so. It is time again for a grand strategy, addressing stability and freedom in the Asia-Pacific region, this time for the twenty – first century.

---

[2] Hal Brands, *The Promise and Pitfalls of Grand Strategy*, (Carlisle, PA: U.S. Army War College, Strategic Studies Institute Publications, 2012), 3.

[3] Willianson Murray and Mark Grimsley, *The Making of Strategy, Rulers, States, and War*, (Cambridge: Cambridge University Press, 1994), I.

[4] Michael Howard, "Grand Strategy in the Twentieth Century," *Defence Studies* 1, no. 1 (Spring 2001): 1.

[5] Grand strategy definitions can be found in the works of Paul Kennedy, Stephen Biddle, Sir Michael Howard, and Martha Crenshaw.

After 1950, the United States developed a grand strategy through an understanding of the strategic environment with clearly articulated and understood ends, supported by a realistic construction of ways, and a careful assessment of means. This strategy document, known as NSC-68, guided U.S. policy throughout the Cold War. NSC-68 continues to be the example of how a grand strategy should be formulated.

NSC-68

In April of 1950, President Harry S. Truman issued a tasking: "the President directs the Secretary of State and Secretary of Defense to undertake a reexamination of our objectives in peace and war and the effect of these objectives on our strategic plans...."[6] The product of this review was the then classified document NSC-68. As it aligned the nation's strategic plans with desired end states, based on enduring American interests, the NSC-68 recommendations became the foundation of a U.S. grand strategy.

The nation's values and ideals that defined the strategic ends were clearly articulated and derived from the U.S. Constitution and the Declaration of Independence.[7] The strategic ways were defined in political, psychological, economic, and military terms. NSC-68 also addressed the means needed to sustain such a strategy, and identified risks. Although the need for such a grand strategy today is less urgent because the United

---

[6] Office of the Executive Secretary to the President, *A Report to the National Security Council - NSC 68*, 14 April 1950, (Washington DC: Government Printing Office), 3. Document found online via National Archives and Records Administration. "Ideological Foundations of the Cold War." Harry S. Truman Library and Museum. http://www.trumanlibrary.org/whistlestop/study_collections/coldwar/documents/pdf/10-1.pdf. (accessed February 22, 2013).

[7] Ibid, 5.

States faces no existential threat from another state or actor, nevertheless, the strategic necessity of has returned. While America's ends have not dramatically changed since NSC-68, the strategic environment has changed significantly. A careful assessment of the post-Cold War strategic environment in Asia is necessary before traditional ends can be balanced with current ways and means.

In 2012 the president and the secretary of defense produced a document entitled "Sustaining U.S. Global Leadership." It appears to be intended to guide U.S. strategy for the next twenty years. The document, endorsed by the president, is intended to "identify our strategic interests."[8] Unlike the grand strategy of NSC-68, both the 2010 National Security Strategy and its 2012 update have a mismatch between ends, ways, means, and risk.

A senior defense specialist speaking under anonymity admitted the United States cannot resource all the desired ends from the 2010 National Security Strategy and the latest update conforms to budget realities rather than conforming to national ends.[9] Other senior leaders in the Office of the Secretary of Defense state the 2012 document is not a national security strategy, but purely guidance. The president signaled his intent that the 2012 document should inform and shape the Joint Force for 2020 and beyond, implying guidance rather than strategy.[10]

In 1950, American policy makers and strategists understood the strategic environment in the aftermath of the Second World War and developed a grand strategy

---

[8] Obama, *Sustaining U.S. Global Leadership*, cover letter.

[9] The use of senior defense officials is used many times in this paper. Information obtained from these sources was given in non-attributional environments or under other cases of anonymity.

[10] Obama, *Sustaining U.S. Global Leadership,* 1.

based on ends, ways, means, and risk. A similar effort is needed for the remaining decades of the twenty – first century. Before any effort is taken, the strategic environment must be assessed. In addition, the desired outcome of this Asia-Pacific rebalance strategy must be clearly articulated, along with the ways, balanced by the means. A full understanding of the requirements for national security strategy, strategic modeling and established common terms of reference is necessary. Without this strategic model, the United States risks the danger of misreading intent and fighting an unnecessary war in Asia and creating an unnecessary adversary.

CHAPTER 1: THE IMPERATIVE OF A GRAND STRATEGY

NATIONAL STRATEGY AND LEGAL REQUIREMENTS

"The doctrinal approach to foreign policy doesn't make much sense anymore."[1]

Fareed Zakaria's comment above reflects a view that in a post-Cold War, multipolar world, foreign policy defined as a doctrine is a fallacy.[2] Whether one currently sees the world as multipolar or unipolar (with the U.S. as the dominant power) does not matter. The United States should have a grand strategy steeped in strategic theory; otherwise decision making in Asia will be reactive, uncoordinated, and confusing. The United States will potentially squander it resources to gain nothing.

A movement away from this view in the post-Cold War period and one toward more of reaction based policy has left the nation without a successful model for grand strategy. Since the end of the Cold War, the United States has made strategy a political tool, crafted largely to favor the interests of the current administration, leading to a tendency to react to events, rather than guiding outcomes. Leon Panetta, the Secretary of Defense, in 2013 articulated these concerns to America's political leadership and the American public. Both in Congressional testimony and in public speeches, the message is that the United States has devolved into a country capable of dealing only in crisis. Its strategy is reactive.[3] Secretary Panetta's comments referred to the current sequestration

---

[1] Fareed Zakaria, "Stop Searching for an Obama Doctrine," *The New York Times*, July 6, 2011.

[2] Ibid.

[3] Secretary Leon Panetta, address to Georgetown University, 6 February 2013. http://www.defense.gov/Transcripts/Transcript.aspx?TranscriptID=5189 (accessed February 22, 2013). Additionally, Secreatary Panetta made similar comments during his testimony to the Senate Armed Services Committee on 7 February available online at http://www.c-spanvideo.org/program/310872-1.

uncertainty, but he was also criticizing the politically reactive behavior that has become the normal way Washington deals with difficult strategic challenges.[4]

The ultimate purpose when developing a nation's grand strategy is for the survival of the nation. Grand strategy is developed "in accordance with a more structured and coherent idea of what their nation is out to accomplish in international affairs."[5]

Some research, including work done by Hal Brands, argues a grand strategy does not have to be "formally enunciated and defined."[6] Additionally, it also argues that nation–states all have a sort of grand strategy, whether they articulate one with a well thought–out theory, or just let the environment operate around them it will still define them and ultimately be their grand strategy. Brands argues that a series of unconnected or reactive measures can serve as a grand strategy, albeit a poor grand strategy. Grand strategy must be thought out carefully. Thus, Brands indicates that recent U.S. national security strategies (including the 2012 update) are marginal or poor grand strategies. There is danger, however, in even calling these recent national security strategies a grand strategy. Just because a nation state makes choices based on interests, it is not a grand strategy, it is as Panetta called it, a reactive approach.

With this reactive approach, the United States must rely almost exclusively on the military as the primary element of power to conduct foreign policy, leaving military leaders without the strategic aims to guide the employment of forces. Beyond pure military objectives, the strategic ends are unknown; far worse, the nation's senior leaders cannot articulate what is to be achieved with the use of force. Given the lack of strategic

---

[4] Ibid.

[5] Hal Brands, *The Promise and Pitfalls of Grand Strategy*, (Carlisle, PA: U.S. Army War College, Strategic Studies Institute Publications, 2012), 3.

[6] Ibid.

interest and a neglect of the strategic art, the overall effect has been presidents in a near-continuous crisis decision mode, or more significantly, reacting to strategic surprise, much as the 2001 terrorist attack, North Korea's nuclear weapons development and testing, ethnic cleansing in Bosnia, genocide in Rwanda, and the Arab Spring.

The source of this problem can be traced to a statutory law that sets the national security strategy timeline *requirement* for the executive branch. According to the National Security Act of 1947, supplemented by Goldwater-Nichols Act of 1986, the president is required to submit a national security strategy annually with the following additional requirements[7]:

- The worldwide interests, goals, and objectives of the United States that are vital to the national security of the United States.[8]

- The foreign policy, worldwide commitments, and national defense capabilities of the United States necessary to deter aggression and to implement the national security strategy of the United States.[9]

- The proposed short-term and long-term uses of the political, economic, military, and other elements of the national power of the United States to protect or promote the interests and achieve the goals and objectives referred to in paragraph.[10]

- The adequacy of the capabilities of the United States to carry out the national security strategy of the United States, including an evaluation of the balance among the capabilities of all elements of the national power of the United States to support the implementation of the national security strategy.[11]

---

[7] Congressional Research Service, *National Security Strategy: Legislative Mandates, Execution to Date, and Considerations for Congress, Dec 15 2008*, (Washington DC: Government Printing Office, 2008), 3.

[8] Ibid.

[9] Ibid.

[10] Ibid.

[11] Ibid.

- Such other information as may be necessary to help inform the Congress on matters relating to the national security strategy of the United States.[12]

While the congressional requirements are in place to hold the executive accountable for national strategy and linking ends, ways, means, and risk, one should assess the utility of this requirement as written. The requirement for ends is cryptically identified in the legal verbiage; nevertheless, ends can be identified as the goals, and objectives vital to national security. Additionally, one can interpret another explicit end as deterring aggression against the United States. The ways requirements that are expressed by the law are to explain the use of foreign policy as well as the short and long term uses of political, economic, military, and other elements of national power. A means requirement is only discussed in the reference of identifying national defense capabilities to implement the strategy. Finally, the requirement to identify risk can be interpreted by the requirement to explain the adequacy of the capabilities to include the evaluation of balance among the elements of national power.

From a strategic theory perspective the law mandates the executive branch articulate the appropriate key elements of strategy, but the timeline requirement to produce the strategy is flawed. Each administration has tailored its national security strategy to its own political needs. Instead of a formulation of strategy, it is becoming increasingly common for administrations to highly politicize the NSS and not to adhere to the congressional timelines.[13] The eminent strategist Harry Yarger states that strategy has a

---

[12] Ibid.

[13] Ibid.

9

"symbiotic relationship with time."[14] A timeline mandated by Congress should not drive

strategy development. Instead, as Yarger notes, "strategy is concerned with continuities

and change."[15] To merely put a deliverable date on a nation's strategy (grand or

otherwise) results in the development of a document resembling strategy shaped by

politics and policy, serving more of a role as planning guidance. Yarger reminds us that

"strategy is about thinking and acting in time in a way that is fundamentally different

from planning."[16]

Nor have previous administrations followed the Congressional requirements, from a

timeline perspective as well as an ends, ways, means, risk perspective. Starting with

George W. Bush and continuing on with Barack Obama, there has been little adherence

to the law. Since 2001 only three national security strategies have been produced: 2002

and 2006.[17] The current administration's last National Security Strategy was published in

2010, but it was almost certainly drafted in 2009.

The primary focus for the 2010 National Security Strategy was "renewing American

leadership so that we can more effectively advance our interests in the 21st century."[18]

Yet under the 2010 document's strategic approach, leadership is not the focus area, but

rather economic power; "Our prosperity serves as the well spring for our power…it pays

for our military, underwrites our diplomacy and development efforts, and serves as a

---

[14] Harry R. Yarger, *The Little Book on Big Strategy* (Carlisle, PA: U.S. Army War College, Strategic Studies Institute Publications, 2006), 13, 68.

[15] Ibid, 13.

[16] Ibid, 68.

[17] National Security Strategy Archive. "National Security Strategy Reports." National Security Strategy Archive, http://nssarchive.us/, (accessed April 24 2013).

[18] President Barack Obama, *National Security Strategy*, (Washington DC: Government Printing Office May 2010), 1.

leading source of influence in the world."[19] The legal requirement is to identify the adequacy of the capabilities of the United States to carry out the national security strategy is ignored. There is little mention of what actions the U.S. has taken or will take to ensure the capabilities meet the requirement.

With poor guidance for strategy formulation, a yearly requirement, and a lack of understanding the strategic environment, it is not surprising that America's national security strategy is highly politicized and often late. The next chapter produces a brief overview of the strategic art and a model of strategy formulation. Using Harry Yarger's strategic model and his strategic principles, it will illustrate the value of grand strategy by applying Yarger's outline to NSC-68.

---

[19] Ibid, 9.

CHAPTER 2: A REVIEW OF THE FOUNDATIONS OF STRATEGY

"Strategy for the nation-state is neither simple nor easy. Good strategy demands much . . . . Few do it well."[1]

The influential strategist, Harry Yarger defines strategy as "the calculation of objectives, concepts and resources within acceptable bounds of risk to create more favorable outcomes that might otherwise exist by chance or at the hands of others."[2] Grand strategy is implemented to influence the environment in order to achieve desired ends. Yarger asserts that strategy formulation must be driven by an understanding of the strategic environment. Yarger's definition used objectives, concepts, and resources – a more succinct and corresponding expression of these ideas is ends, ways, means, and risk. Henry Bartlett also uses similar terms in his similar strategic model in which strategy sits atop a continuous loop linking goals (ends), tools (means), and risk.[3] Additionally, Bartlett's model is influenced by two injects; resource constraints and the security environment (also to be understood as the strategic environment).[4]

Once the strategic environment is defined, understood, and assessed, clearly defined end states can be determined based on enduring values or longer-term strategic conditions. This will, in essence, be the ends of an emerging grand strategy. Ideally, grand strategy is supported by sub-strategies; policies are subordinate and at the center

---

[1] Yarger, ix.

[2] Ibid, 1.

[3] Henry C. Bartlett, G. Paul Holman Jr., and Timothy E. Somes, "The Art of Strategy and Force Planning," *Srategy and Force Planning, 4ᵗʰ Ed*, (Newport, RI: Naval War College Press , 2004), 18-19.

[4] Ibid.

are clearly articulated ends, ways, and means, while accounting for risk.[5] Before

examining the ends, ways, means construct in further detail, it is essential to review the

external and internal factors that will influence a given strategy – they are the factors

make up the strategic environment.

STRATEGIC ENVIRONMENT

Yarger states that "both strategy and planning are subordinate to the nature of the

environment."[6] The environment is dynamic and entails many facets for consideration.

Strategist Colin Gray characterizes the strategic environment as one of friction, chance,

and uncertainty. In addition, Gray has articulated these with others to form seventeen key

areas that should be considered when defining the strategic environment.[7] These

seventeen dimensions apply both internally and externally.

From an internal perspective, each of these dimensions has potential effects

within the state itself, as they relate to the internal environment of the state. Externally

the effects in the environment are based on other interactions without necessarily a

strategic input from the nation's grand strategy. It could be compared to a science

experiment, where there is the control group (internal) and the variable group (external).

While not necessarily all-inclusive, Gray's dimensions can guide the understanding of the

strategic environment and set the stage for strategy development in a constant assessment

process.

---

[5] Ibid, 11, 67.

[6] Yarger, 5.

[7] Colin S. Gray, "RMAs and the Demensions of Strategy," Joint Forces Quarterly (Autmn/Winter 1997-98): 50. The seveteen dimensions are as follows: ethics; society; geography; politics; people; culture; theory; command; economics and logistics; organization; military preparation; operations; technology; information and intelligence; adversary; friction, chance, uncertainty; and time.

Yarger sums up the strategic environment in four factors: volatility, uncertainty, complexity, and ambiguity. Yarger emphasizes the need to see through the chaos and being comfortable operating within chaotic states of the environment as essential to good strategy development. [8] Assessing the strategic environment will reveal a level of chaos that the strategists must accept and still be able to develop strategy that works effectively within the chaos. Yarger believes that strategists must also consider alternate futures. Further expounding on the inherent chaos of the strategic environment, Mackubin Thomas Owens states that strategy "is a process, a constant adaptation to shifting conditions and circumstances in a world where chance, uncertainty, and ambiguity dominate."[9]

The architects of NSC-68 were able to assess and articulate the complex environment clearly. In laying out the external environment, NSC-68 explained the roots of the current strategic environment as well as the conditions that defined the emerging global structure of the Cold War:

> Within the past thirty-five years the world has experienced two wars of tremendous violence. It has witnessed two revolutions—the Russian and the Chinese—of extreme scope and intensity. It was also seen the collapse of five empires—the Ottoman, the Austro-Hungarian, German, Italian and Japanese—and the drastic decline of two major imperial systems, the British and the French. . . .For several centuries it had proved impossible for any one nation to gain such preponderant strength that a coalition of other nations could not in time face it with greater strength.[10]

After framing the historical perspective, NSC-68 further described the current state of world affairs:

---

[8] Yarger, 17-18.

[9] Ibid.

[10] Office of the Executive Secretary to the President, *A Report to the National Security Council - NSC 68*, 4.

> Two complex set of factors have now basically altered this historic distribution of power. First the defeat of Germany and Japan and the decline of British and French Empires have interacted with the development of the United States and the Soviet Union in such a way that power increasingly gravitated to these two centers. Second, the Soviet Union, unlike previous aspirants to hegemony, is animated by a new fanatic faith, antithetical to our own and seeks to impose its absolute authority over the rest of the world.[11]

From the NSC-68 extract above, uncertainty and friction are clearly identified by the acknowledgement of four major world powers are in collapse, a new world order of a bi-polar system is emerging with an enemy that has unseen hegemonic aspirations not witnessed before.

Taking Gray's factors, NSC-68 also provides evidence of internal environmental assessment. Recognizing that any strategic assessment must be acceptable to the American people and any strategy implemented must be "only through the traditional democratic process."[12] Furthermore, it was recognized that the American people must each understand the issues, formulate their own opinions and communicate their choices to their elected officials. NSC-68 assessed vulnerabilities to implementing such a strategy.

> A free society is vulnerable in that it is easy for people to lapse into excesses – the excesses of a permanently open mind wishfully waiting for evidence that evil design may become a noble purpose, the excess of faith becoming prejudice, the excess of tolerance degenerating into the indulgence of conspiracy and the excess of resorting to suppression when more moderate measures are not only more appropriate, but more effective.[13]

Understanding the strategic environment is critical to frame perspective. From this perspective key factors emerge in NSC-68. These key factors were: Germany's defeat and division in Europe, Japan's defeat and destruction in Asia and the collapse of

---

[11] Ibid.

[12] Ibid, 23.

[13] Ibid.

the French and British colonial based empires. Furthermore, based on those previous key factors, the post-World War II strategic environment was set for the Soviet Union to assume power and become a threat as traditional anchors of security and power became less capable. This new and different threat emerged that challenged the very essence of democracy and a free society.

ENDS

Yarger states: "In strategy formulation, getting the objectives (ends) right matters most!"[14] Once the strategic environment is defined, understood, and assessed, clearly defined end states should be determined based on enduring values or long-term strategic conditions. A key part of assessing ends correctly is articulating *why* these ends are the paramount.[15] NSC-68 clearly laid out the end state to protect the American way of life; "to maintain the essential elements of individual freedom, as set forth in the Constitution and Bill of Rights; create conditions under which our free and democratic system can live and prosper."[16]

Ends should be understood and articulated in terms of shaping the current environment. In NSC-68 the root issue was an existential threat to U.S. survival. "The [Soviet] design, therefore, calls for the complete subversion or forcible destruction of the machinery of government and structure of society in the countries of the non-Soviet world."[17] The entire strategy was devised to counter communism, as it did threaten

---

[14] Yarger, 48.

[15] Ibid.

[16] Office of the Executive Secretary to the President, *A Report to the National Security Council - NSC 68*, 5.

[17] Ibid, 6.

America's physical existence and the U.S. way of life. NSC-68 identified three clear objectives which Yarger also calls ends.[18] The first of these three objectives were to "make [the U.S.] strong; through affirmation of values in the American way of life, militarily, and economically."[19] Second, within this strategy NSC-68 stated America must "lead in building a successfully functioning political and economic system in the free world."[20] The final objective NSC-68 identified was to foster a fundamental change in the nature of the Soviet system."[21]

As Yarger indicates, strategy must not be reactive, but enduring. NSC-68 acknowledges this idea in the following concept; "there is no reason, in the event of war, for us to alter our overall objectives."[22] Neither end state nor shaping effects would have to be modified in case of war with the Soviet Union, thus meeting Yarger's requirement that ends must be comprehensive yet reflect an appreciation for the fundamental nature of the strategic environment "to allow change in execution with losing focus on policy or interests."[23] Ends, therefore, are understood in relation to the strategic environment.

Furthermore, the objectives led to articulated desired end states, ways of implementation, and then focused U.S. resources to achieve the desired ends. As Yarger states, getting the ends right is the imperative of grand strategy, as all else is based on achieving those ends. With well articulated strategic ends, the next question(s) to answer

---

[18] Yarger, 48.

[19] Office of the Executive Secretary to the President, *A Report to the National Security Council - NSC 68*, 9.

[20] Ibid.

[21] Ibid.

[22] Ibid, 10.

[23] Yarger, 53.

are the possible mechanisms available to the nation to pursue the ends. These mechanisms are known in strategic theory as the ways.

WAYS

*"The logic of strategy argues that the strategic concept answers the big question of **how** the objectives will be achieved..."*[24]

Developing ways is the next step of strategy; it connects the appropriate resources to achieve the desired ends. Ways should be thought of as the how a strategy is to be accomplished. Ways must also be thought-out carefully because if incorrect ways are applied to achieve the ends, there will be a misallocation of resources and the ends will not be achieved.

Understanding balance of the ways is critical in utilizing the instruments of national power. Paul Kennedy captures optimizing the instruments of power as "the crux of grand strategy lies therefore in policy, that is, in the capacity of the nation's leaders to bring together all of the elements, both military and nonmilitary, for the preservation and enhancement of the nation's long term best interests"[25] What is important to understand from Kennedy is that in grand strategy it is the blend or combination of the instruments of power in harmony that offer the best chance of success in achieving the ends. Scholars may refer to the specific categories in an array of terms, but a common set of terms are known as the DIME; Diplomatic, Information, Military, and Economic and can be thought in in the following way. "Instruments of power are the manifestation of the

---

[24] Yarger, 60.

[25] Paul Kennedy, "Grand Strategy in War and Peace: Toward a Broader Definition," in Paul Kennedy, ed., *Grand Strategies in War and Peace*, (New Haven: Yale University Press, 1991), 7.

elements of power (the states resources) in action."[26] Similarly, the DoD dictionary defines instruments of power as "all of the means available to the government in its pursuit of national objectives. They are expressed as DIME: diplomatic (political influence through relationships with other countries or entities (such as the United Nations)), informational (messaging through media or other outlets to establish or win the battle of the narrative), military (the forces and capabilities to use physical force to compel a change of behavior), and economic (uses prosperity or potential prosperity to influence others)."[27] Understanding that all instruments of power should be used as ways in achieving ends is critical when developing strategy.

NSC-68 viewed the diplomatic instrument of power as the ability to influence other world actors through relationships that were being fostered with non-Soviet controlled states in Western Europe, Latin America, Asia, and Africa.[28] The approach that emerged out of NSC-68 was twofold. First, were diplomatic efforts to "develop the international community"[29] and second was "containing the Soviet system."[30]

NSC-68 used the term psychological ways versus informational ways to describe this aspect of power, but the intent was similar. The message of a free people, given to govern themselves was the cornerstone of this message. With intent to spread the

---

[26] Yarger, 60.

[27] U.S. Joint Chiefs of Staff, *Department of Defense Dictionary of Military and Associated Terms*, Joint Publication 1-02,(Washington DC: Joint Chiefs of Staff, Nov 8 2010), 138.

[28] Office of the Executive Secretary to the President, *A Report to the National Security Council - NSC 68*, 24.

[29] Ibid, 21.

[30] Ibid.

message throughout the free world as well as to show and inspire the Soviet people a more favorable way of life.[31]

NSC-68 pointed out the need for a strong military to support the overall strategy not necessarily to pursue combat the Soviet Union in action, but rather to take "the potential military capabilities...to deter war, or if the Soviet Union chooses war, to withstand the initial Soviet attacks, to stabilize supporting attacks, and to retaliate in turn with even greater impact on the Soviet capabilities."[32]

While many might quickly be drawn to the military superiority as the determining factor in winning the Cold War, economic power was the principle way articulated in NSC-68. "Foreign economic policy is a major instrument in the conduct of United States foreign relations."[33] NSC-68 identified the value of both internal economic prosperity and bolstering allies and partners using the economic instrument of power. NSC-68 stressed that "it is an instrument peculiarly appropriate to the cold war."[34]

These instruments of national power must be synchronized with the ends. The ways feed the ends. Therefore, when developing grand strategy, not only do the ways need to be in line to serve the ends, but they must also have adequate resources for the ways to be effective. As Yarger states, "The responsibility of the strategist is to ensure that the resources necessary for the accomplishment of the objectives as envisioned by the concepts are articulated and available."[35]

---

[31] Office of the Executive Secretary to the President, *A Report to the National Security Council - NSC 68*, 7.

[32] Ibid, 32.

[33] Ibid, 28.

[34] Ibid.

[35] Yarger, 60.

MEANS

"Resource selection, like concepts, has implications in regard to multi-level effects"[36]

Means are the resources available by which the ways achieve the ends. Resources are not unlimited in whatever form and therefore are always constrained.

In the aftermath of World War II, the United States was in a period of dramatic budget reductions. Although military capability was not at a level deemed acceptable for the NSC-68 strategy, the strategists accounted for what was required, and then sought to resource that requirement. Yarger explains this is perfectly acceptable in strategy formulation. "A national security or grand strategy could list 'military forces' as a resource for its concepts, even if the appropriate types of forces did not exist, and still be consistent as long as the development of the forces was funded and the concept allow the time for building the force."[37]

Resource constraints should also be in discussion when accounting for risk; for if risk is not included in the cross check of strategy development, the ends-ways-means portion of the model will not hold for very long.

RISK

Yarger states that beyond the simple calculation of winning and losing, "risk assessment is...an assessment of the probable consequences of success and failure."[38] Accounting for risk is only useful if it is understood and assessed. Strategists should envision what in the environment could influence the current assessment of risk. Yarger explains risk in validating strategy in these terms:

---

[36] Ibid 61.

[37] Ibid.

[38] Ibid, 63.

Risk…seeks to determine what effects are created by the implementation of the strategy. Is seeks to determine how the equilibrium is affected, and whether the environment is more or less favorable for the state as a result of the strategy.[39]

Appropriate risk assessment assists with prioritization, weight of effort and resource allocation. If risk is unacceptable and requires mitigation, often ways or resources are redirected to reduce the risk. Understanding the risk will assist strategists with what are the most important key factors to the strategic environment. From that a prioritization of resources to address the most important issues should occur. Weight of effort can be captured as a measure of how much time, resources, or political commitment should be spent on a certain area. Allocation is the actual execution of resources to further the strategy.

NSC-68 gives much attention to risk and assessment of risk. Including sub risks with each of the ways (political, physiological, military, and economic) NSC-68 devotes an entire chapter to a holistic risk assessment–both in risk to America if no action was taken as well as the risk in bolstering the United States to counter Soviet aggression:

> there are risks to making ourselves strong. A large measure of sacrifices and discipline will be demanded of the American people….They will be asked to give up some of the benefits which they have come to associate with their freedoms. The risks of a superficial understand or of an inadequate appreciate of the issues are obvious and might lead to the adoption of measures which in themselves would jeopardize the integrity of our system.[40]

NSC-68 articulated that even if the recommended course of action was taken there would be risk to achieving national support as well as once the support of the population was behind the strategy that it could take such a fanatical turn that it would be counter to what the strategy was set out to do.

---

[39] Ibid.

[40] Office of the Executive Secretary to the President, *A Report to the National Security Council - NSC 68*, 36.

Thus far this chapter has discussed certain key attributes of strategy formulation such as understanding the strategic environment, identifying interests and in-turn strategic ends, ways, means and risk. Just as Gray has seventeen dimensions to help understand and frame the strategic environment, Yarger has principles to help with the understanding and formulating grand strategy.

YARGER'S PRICIPLES OF STRATEGY

Yarger has fifteen principles of strategy, all driving back to supporting the ends, ways, means and risk construct. The following highlights some of these principles as they relate directly to this analysis. In analyzing the NSC-68 grand strategy several key principles stand out.

Political purpose dominates all strategy

> At the dawn of the 21st century, our world is very different from that of our Founding Fathers, yet the basic objectives in the preamble to the Constitution remain timeless: Provide for the common defense, promote the general welfare, and secure the blessings of liberty to ourselves and our posterity.
>
> -   President Clinton, 2001 NSS

A grand strategy should be based on longstanding political beliefs and enduring end states. In other words, a grand strategy should be able to survive the United States political system and the end states should be enduring regardless of a democrat or republican leadership. NSC-68 clearly listed out the enduring principles of maintaining key basis of freedom, provide an environment where the democratic system can thrive, and defend the American way of life.[41]

Strategy is subordinate to the nature of the strategic environment

---

[41] Ibid, 5.

One must consider and understand the environment before developing grand strategy. "Strategy must be consistent with the nature of the strategic environment in its formulation and execution."[42] This analysis should include state and non-state actors, relevancy, political or international power, and contextual history. Colin Gray's seventeen principles help to qualify what is contained in the strategic environment as a framework, but the strategist must be able to glean salient points from the principles to logically tie them to the greater strategic effort.

Amidst the post-World War II chaos, NSC-68 clearly laid out the strategic environment. "The 'peace policy' of the Soviet Union…is a device to divide and immobilize the non-Communist world, and the peace the Soviet Union seeks is the peace of total conformity to Soviet policy."[43] It was this assault on freedom and free will that permeated every aspect of the strategic environment. Relooking events in history, NSC-68 further expounded about the central issue as "the idea of freedom is the most contagious idea in history, more contagious than the idea of submission to authority."[44]

Strategy is grounded in *what* is to be accomplished and *why* it is to be accomplished

At each step of strategic thought, one should be able to clearly tie back actions that support the ends. If one cannot in any point of strategy formulation articulate why actions are being taken, the strategy is flawed and can cause actions that are irrelevant and arguably costly to desired outcomes of the strategy. NSC-68 provided four strategic options for the United States to take given the strategic environment and desired end states. Those were the status quo approach, retrenchment, go to war, or "the remaining

---

[42] Yarger, 8.

[43] Office of the Executive Secretary to the President, *A Report to the National Security Council - NSC 68*, 8.

[44] Ibid.

course of action – a rapid build-up of political, economic, and military strength in the free world."[45] Each course of action assessed Yarger's principle of what and why the course of action would be executed. These options were assessed through the lenses of the military, political, economic and social; essentially the DIME method. While each of the courses of action had portions of the DIME that could marginally satisfy the desired ends, only the rapid build-up across the free world satisfied what was to be done and why said option was required. It was well argued that this option "by confidence of the free world…is the only course which is consistent with progress toward achieving our fundamental purpose."[46]

Strategy is proactive and anticipatory

> *- Strategy is not crisis management. It is to a large degree its antithesis.*[47]

One must be aware grand strategy, should be enduring and not subject to dramatic changes. The strategy should be structured that only modest adjustments are necessary. NSC-68 was designed to counter the threat from Soviet domination, "it is not an adequate objective merely to seek to check the Kremlin design…in our own interests, the responsibility of world leadership."[48] The strategy did not change from a single event; rather it guided decision making for the appropriate use of the instruments of power that the United States would use both to counter the Soviet threat as well as to improve the security and prosperity of America as a whole. In other words, this strategy did more

---

[45] Ibid, 48-54.

[46] Ibid, 54.

[47] Yarger, 6.

[48] Office of the Executive Secretary to the President, *A Report to the National Security Council - NSC 68*, 9.

than just counter every Soviet activity; it also proactively utilized American instruments of national power for the betterment of the United States and the entire free world.

The first step in formulating strategy is understanding and assessing the strategic environment. Yarger's strategy model is one that follows a logical equation that starts with desired ends and then determines ways to achieve the ends. The ways must be adequately resourced or the strategy will not be effective. Risk assessment is critical for good strategy. Good strategy lays out the possibilities in advance and allows for flexibility based on the outcomes encountered. Additionally the strategist must assess how the environment will react when the desired ends and ways are pursued to achieve specific ends. NSC-68 serves as a solid backdrop of supporting Yarger's strategy development theory. With an understanding of what good strategy looks like based on sound strategic principles and model for strategy formulation, the current national security strategy of 2010 and its subsequent 2012 update will be examined and analyzed.

CHAPTER 3: CURRENT STRATEGY: AN ASSESSMENT

The previous chapter has provided a strategic model and used NSC-68 as an example of grand strategy. This chapter will analyze the current document that is understood as the national security strategy. First, in accordance with Yarger's model, it will identify the strategic environment as listed in the document, and then extract the ends, ways, means and any articulation of risk. This will provide the basis for a detailed analysis and assessment of the current strategic document using the same four principles of Yarger's principles of strategy from the previous chapter.

The U.S. security strategy document, "Sustaining U.S. Global Leadership: Priorities for 21st Century Defense," is an amalgam of other security documents residing in security strategy development, planning, and execution. It signed by the President, yet the document has the stamp of the Office of the Secretary of Defense, creating uncertainty as to whether or not the update represents a national security strategy.

There was no national security strategy published in 2011, as required by law, and no specific document titled National Security Strategy was published in 2012. However, it is logical when one begins to read the security document published in January 2012, this was the next attempt of a security strategy by the administration.

> This strategic guidance document describes the projected security environment and the key military missions for which the Department of Defense will prepare. It is intended as a blueprint for the Joint Force in 2020, providing a set of precepts that will help guide decisions regarding the size and shape of the force over subsequent program and budget cycles, and highlighting some of the strategic risks that may be associated with the proposed strategy.[1]

The above uses terms that are associated with strategy, but falls short in laying out other key pieces of strategy. As Yarger and others have discussed, understanding the

---

[1] Obama, *Sustaining U.S. Global Leadership*, 1.

environment is fundamental in strategy development. The summary above does address environment. Ways are only mentioned regarding the military; means are briefly touched on with regard to resourcing and risk is only mentioned once in the 2012 update.[2] Further discussion in this chapter will examine how well the document addresses these portions of strategy. However, in the documents overview paragraph above, there is no mention of ends.

STRATEGIC ENVIRONMENT

Through review of the document as compared to strategic theory, one can examine its assessment of the strategic environment. The following highlights what the document considers the environmental factors. The 2012 strategy document does a sufficient job of articulating the strategic environment.

The document accurately assesses the internal factor that the U.S. is fiscally constrained after fighting two wars over the past decade.[3] It is unquestioned that a decade of conflict along with a worldwide economic downturn, would severely limit resources available.

There is an appreciation for the ongoing instability in the Middle East, which manifested itself in the Arab Spring. This multi-nation revolution has witnessed uprisings in Egypt, Libya, Tunisia and the ongoing civil war in Syria. Oppression of universal rights of these nations' populations is highlighted in the 2012 document.[4]

Without question other state and non-state actors play a significant threat to the world as the document states, "Al Qaida and terrorist non-state actors remain active in

---

[2] Ibid, 8.

[3] Ibid, cover letter.

[4] Ibid.

Pakistan, Afghanistan, Yemen, and Somalia."[5] The document accurately assesses that Iran continues to threaten neighboring countries and remains a large factor of instability (highlighted by its quest for a nuclear weapon) in the Middle East.[6]

Europe is described as a "home to some of America's most stalwart allies."[7] Additionally, Europe is labeled as the primary partnership of importance for both economics and worldwide stability, yet it also recognizes that Europe is also in the midst of economic crisis and discusses that many NATO countries have dramatically reduced their military budgets.[8]

The next several environmental factors examine areas that influence American interests. "Economic and security interests are inextricably linked to developments in the arc extending from the Western Pacific and East Asia into the Indian Ocean region and South Asia, creating a mix of challenges and opportunities."[9] One of the opportunities the document identifies is India's growth which has signaled a rising power in Asia that the U.S. seeks to build partnership[10] The ongoing security dilemma with North Korea continues despite pressures and sanctions from the international community.[11] North Korea exists as a Cold War relic, although its nuclear weapons program troubles its traditional supporters, China and Russia.

---

[5] Ibid, 1.

[6] Ibid.

[7] Ibid, 2.

[8] Ibid, 3. The document also refers to the concept of "Smart Defense" which is a capabilities segmented concept around which nations develop their militaries. In essence countries are considering if not already abdicated some of their sovereignty by having other nations cover their defense requirements.

[9] Ibid, 2.

[10] Ibid.

[11] Ibid, 2-3.

Finally, the 2012 update identifies China's influence on U.S. economic prosperity and security. Without question, China has grown its economic power over the last thirty years. Globalization has intertwined the economies of the United States and China although "the growth of China's military power" the document emphasizes, "must be accompanied by greater clarity of its strategic intentions."[12]

In strategic assessment, as Yarger states, "context always matters...ultimately the success of the strategic effects depends on what the adversary and others choose to do and on what reality turns out to be."[13] The document makes an effort to provide an assessment of the strategic environment, identifying threats, friends, and adversaries. China, unlike Iran or North Korea is in a very ambiguous position. The U.S. apparently has no clear idea whether China is a friend or foe. There appears to be a wait-and-see approach. Also, there is no reflection of dynamic change – The world system appears rather static. While U.S. resolve to have presence in the Pacific has not changed in twenty years, the strategic environment has changed. Understanding the strategic environment in the context of enduring national interests will help identify desired ends.

ENDS

The next step in good strategy formulation is how the U.S. is to operate in that environment in order to achieve desired ends. The 2012 document provides the: Freedom of access, prevention of a nuclear armed North Korea and Iran, regional security, and renewed economic strength as ends.[14] However, these ends are not overtly stated as ends and had to be extracted through thorough examination. The 2010 National

---

[12] Ibid, 2-5.

[13] Yarger, 45.

[14] Obama, *Sustaining U.S. Global Leadership*, cover letter.

Security Strategy ends are also not clearly articulated. The 2010 document clearly identifies America's interests: security, prosperity, values, and international order. Interests are not ends. It then proceeds directly into ways to use the national instruments of power without first clearly identifying the desired ends.[15] These ends are both broad and narrow lacking clarity necessary to apply ends and ways.

WAYS AND MEANS

The ways identified in the 2012 document are almost exclusively military. Although the document gives insight into "strengthen[ing] all the tools of American power, including diplomacy and development, intelligence, and homeland security,"[16] there is not an in-depth discussion on these other adapted forms of the instruments of power. Intelligence and Homeland Security are curious additions. They are not further addressed, nor clearly defined. Diplomacy, a classic instrument of power is linked to development – a term also not defined. The vagueness illustrates merely political jargon *not* strategic thinking. Recall Yarger's definition of ways: as they "explain 'how' the objectives are to be accomplished by the employment of the instruments of power."[17] The document does not specifically define means to achieve ill-defined ends.

The military instrument of power is provided with specific mission sets to achieve ill-defined ends. The joint force mission sets as defined within the document are: deter and defeat aggression; project power despite anti-access/area denial challenges; counter weapons of mass destruction; operate effectively in cyberspace and space; maintain a

---

[15] Obama, *National Security Srategy*, 9, 17-50. As an example in this National Security Strategy, there is a section called the The World We Seek; in this section there is no mention of desired end states only ways. These ways are subsections called Building Our Foundation, Pursuing Comprehensive Engagement, and Promoting a Just and Sustainable International Order.

[16] Obama, *Sustaining U.S. Global Leadership,* cover letter.

[17] Yarger, 55.

safe, secure, and effective nuclear deterrent; defend the homeland and provide civil support; provide a stabilizing presence; conduct stability and counter insurgency operations; and conduct humanitarian, disaster relief and other operations.[18] In other words, the military instrument will do everything to meet the national interests. This is a model of a reactive approach. Any threat becomes a military problem. But because there is no linkage of ends, ways, and means the military is given a list of requirements to fulfill.

- "Deter and Defeat Aggression: Credible deterrence results from both the capabilities to deny an aggressor the prospect of achieving his objectives and from the complementary capability to impose unacceptable costs on the aggressor."[19] (the U.S. military is no longer able to fight two wars simultaneously; it can conduct one major conflict while imposing unacceptable costs on an opportunistic aggressor in a second region. Without specifically stating so, this new posture has risks which go unidentified. Also a new requirement implies that means have changed, also with specific reference to ends.)

- "Project Power Despite Anti-Access/Area Denial Challenges: States such as China and Iran will continue to pursue asymmetric means to counter our power projection capabilities…accordingly, the U.S. military will invest as required to ensure its ability to operate effectively in anti-access and area denial environments."[20] (By placing China in the same hostile threat as Iran is

---

[18] Obama, *Sustaining U.S. Global Leadership*, 4-6.

[19] Ibid.

[20] Ibid, 5.

32

extremely dangerous and counter-productive to the overall end state of economic prosperity. Additionally, it continues the vague strategic assessment of China.)

- "Defend the Homeland and Provide Support to Civil Authorities: We will come to the assistance of domestic civil authorities in the event such defense fails or in case of natural disasters, potentially in response to a very significant or even catastrophic event."[21] (Equally vague – lacking any connections to ends. This document acknowledges the potential failure to defend the homeland.)

- "Provide a Stabilizing Presence: The U.S. will conduct a sustainable pace of presence of stability operations abroad….However, with reduced resources, thoughtful choices will need to be made regarding the location and frequency of these operations."[22] (This is a specific reference to reduced resources yet, the strategy never defines means while it calls for an increase in presence in the largest geographic area of the globe – the Pacific.)

"Conduct Stability and Counterinsurgency Insurgency Operations….U.S. forces will no longer be sized to conduct large scale, prolonged stability operations."[23] (As David Galula notes, to effectively conduct these operations, large forces are

---

[21] Ibid.

[22] Ibid.

[23] Ibid, 6.

required, and required to stay for long periods of time.[24] This is another example of an ends, ways, and means mismatch.)

A majority of the document is spent on identification of these sets as to how they will support the military instrument of power. While not necessarily directly germane to the issues with the pivot to the Pacific, the mission set reflects a complete misapplication of an instrument of national power to accomplish vague and ill-defined ends, and with fewer resources. These mission sets are in no way, shape, or form, prioritized within the strategy.

It identifies ways without sufficient means, illogically directed to the unclear ends. The shift to the Pacific is not justified by the strategic assessment; it is not clear how the national ends are achieved by this shift, and only one instrument of national power is identified. Means are only inferred and risk is completely ignored.

RISK

Finally, in the strategic equation, addressing risk is all but absent from the strategy. Risk is called out only once in the document as is addressed in the following cursory manner. "Force and program decisions made by the Department of Defense will be made in accordance with the strategic approach described in this document, which is designed to ensure our Armed Forces can meet the demands of the National Security Strategy at acceptable risk."[25] What is lacking is a risk assessment that differentiates what is acceptable risk and what is the assessment of overall risk. A March 2012

---

[24] David Galula, *Counterinsurgency Warfare Theory and Practice*, (London: Praeger Publishers, 1964), 4-5. Throughout this work, recurring themes of protracted operations and expense at the cost to the counter insurgent.

[25] Ibid, 8.

Congressional Research Study brings to light one element of risk relating to the

rebalancing approach, which appears to be aimed at China:

> However the widespread perception that the rebalancing initiative is aimed at China also creates a host of risks. The "pivot" to the Pacific is seen by some in China in starker terms, as focused driving China from its neighbors and keeping China's military in check. Such an impression my strengthen the hand of China's military….The military could in turn become more determined to strengthen China's anti-access capabilities and more assertive about defending China's territorial claims rather than less.[26]

The end result, according to the study, is that "it [would be] more difficult for the United

States to gain China's cooperation on such issues as Iran and North Korea."[27] These are

two clearly identified threats in the strategic document neither of which is China.

The study points to risk in the economic realm as well. With China being the

United States' second largest trading partner (first is the European Union), the third

biggest export market, and a holder of substantial U.S. foreign debt, China has substantial

leverage to negate what the Chinese might view as a hostile American intrusion into

Asian affairs.[28] These facts should be addressed at some level and quantified in a risk

analysis. Otherwise, the strategy is flawed – emerging as a political placard rather than a

true strategy.

Another element of risk that the Congressional Report appropriately brings out is

one of other commitments around the globe. As stated in the document, the United States

will still have commitments in the Middle East and Europe, while defining its role in

Africa. The Congressional study observes that:

---

[26] Congressional Research Service, *Pivot to the Pacific? The Obama Administration's "Rebalancing" Toward Asia, Report to Congress, March 2012* (Washington, DC: Government Printing Office, 2012), 8.

[27] Ibid.

[28] Ibid.

Increasing the relative importance of the Asia-Pacific in U.S. policy could conceivably diminish U.S. capabilities in other regions. In particular, in an era of constrained defense resources, an increased U.S. military emphasis on the Asia-Pacific region might result in a reduction in U.S. military presence or capacity in other parts of the worlds, which in turn could increase risks for the United States in those regions. While the United States does not want to reduce its commitments in the Middle East, for instance, forces similar to those needed in Asia are also require there. High priority capabilities in both regions include short-and medium range missile defense, rotational naval deployments and air attack forces, and rapid reaction ground forces. Such forces may be strained by simultaneous demands in both regions.[29]

This glaring gap in the strategic document highlights the troubling mismatch of ends-ways-and means, and leads to the type of instruction found in the document: fight one war while punishing an opportunistic aggressor. As Yarger notes "allocating inadequate resources for a strategic concept is a recipe for disaster, and will cause even greater costs in recovering."[30]

ASSESSMENT

The ends-ways-means construct of sound strategy has been turned on its head: This document reflects a means-driven approach to strategy. In the opening paragraph from the President, his overriding requirement stated that the budget is the preeminent issue; "…we must put our fiscal house in order here at home to renew our long-term economic strength. To that end the Budget Control Act of 2011 mandates reductions in federal spending, including defense spending."[31] The document has resulted in budget policy driving strategy versus strategy leading to policy to support a clearly defined strategy. Yarger states that strategy identifies interests, desired ends then utilizes the instruments of power to achieve those ends; "policy articulates the reflection of these

---

[29] Congressional Research Service, *Pivot to the Pacific?*, 8.

[30] Yarger, 62.

[31] Obama, *Sustaining U.S. Global Leadership*, cover letter.

interests."[32] Additionally, Yarger states that strategy is to inform policy as policy comes out of strategy to meet the strategy's ends.[33] The exact opposite is occurring here – policy is driving strategy.

The new Defense Strategic Guidance lays out many focus areas that can serve as the basis of strategic assessment, Countering Terrorism, China and the Pacific, Iran and nuclear proliferation, Europe and NATO, Building Partner Capacity, Leading the protection of the Global Commons, worldwide proliferation of Weapons of Mass Destruction. Now let us dissect this from a strategic theory perspective starting with root problems and desired end state review.

Yet, the Defense Strategic Guidance includes assurances that the "DoD will manage the force in ways that protect its ability to regenerate capabilities that might be needed to meet future, unforeseen demands, maintaining intellectual capital and rank structure that could be called upon to expand key elements of the force."[34]

One can use Yarger's principles as a litmus test for meeting the requirements of good strategy. As a review it is worthwhile to relook and compare the current strategic document using the same four principles:

Political purpose dominates all strategy

The 2010 National Security Strategy identifies four enduring principles that can be considered congruent to this principle. They are security, prosperity, values, and international order. In the 2012 update these terms are also highlighted in the President's cover letter of the document. However, missing is clear policy that supports ends to these

---

[32] Yarger, 65.

[33] Ibid, 6-7.

[34] President Barack Obama, *Sustaining U.S. Global Leadership,* 6.

enduring American values. As Yarger states, "policy ensures that strategy pursues appropriate aims, while strategy informs policy of the art of the possible."[35]

Strategy is proactive and anticipatory

Within the 2012 update there are indications that this document is a response to an established strategic environment that lacks an appreciation for the dynamic nature of the environment. It is reactive as evidenced in the ways the document goes about implementation. The A2/AD focus is reactive, as is the approach when dealing with North Korea, China, and Iran. The statement "we will of necessity rebalance to the Asia-Pacific"[36] also lends credibility that this is reactionary versus an anticipatory approach.

Strategy is grounded in *what* is to be accomplished and *why* it is to be accomplished

There is no connection for the rebalance to and end state; especially when dealing with the Asia-Pacific, it is unclear as to what is to be accomplished and more importantly why.

Strategy is subordinate to the nature of the strategic environment

While it is acknowledged this document does an acceptable job of understanding the issues within the strategic environment, the strategy does not seem to be connected to the strategic environment review.

In summary the 2012 update to the 2010 national security strategy lacks many key concepts of strategy. While the strategic environmental assessment is sufficient, the remaining parts of strategy development are unclear or missing. There are ends within the 2012 document, but the ways and means do not seem to logically tie back to

---

[35] Yarger, 7.

[36] Obama, *Sustaining U.S. Global Leadership*, 2.

supporting the ends. Furthermore, as indicated in assessment of the 2010 National Security Strategy the ends are not clear, means are vague and the only in-depth portion of strategic development in this document are through the numerous unlinked ways U.S. can project or maintain power. Finally, there is no in-depth acknowledgement or assessment of risk in the 2012 update. This document is considered a strategy, but seems to fail in almost every aspect of Yarger's strategy development model. As the Asia-Pacific is the focal point of this strategy update, the next chapter will specifically dissect that portion of the strategy.

CHAPTER 4: THE PIVOT TO ASIA-UNCLEAR STRATEGIC RATIONALE

PART OF A FLAWED STRATEGY

There is little insight as to why the U.S. is making a fundamental shift to the Asia Pacific region. Looking at the strategic environment now, versus ten to twenty years ago there has not been a fundamental change, save North Korea's progression toward nuclear armament. The origins of this pivot or rebalance goes back to the Clinton administration's 2000 National Security Strategy:

> China's rise as a major power presents an array of potential challenges. Many of China's neighbors are closely monitoring China's growing defense expenditures and modernization of the People's Liberation Army (PLA). Given international and regional focus on China's growing military power, China's adherence to multilateral nonproliferation and arms control regimes, as well as increased military transparency, is of growing importance.[1]

The January 2012 strategy update language is remarkably similar:

> China's emergence as a regional power will have the potential to affect the U.S. economy and our security in a variety of ways. Our two countries have a strong stake in peace and stability in East Asia and an interest in building a cooperative bilateral relationship. However, the growth of China's military power must be accompanied by greater clarity of its strategic intentions in order to avoid causing friction in the region.[2]

Both excerpts focus on China's military power. China is described in 2000 as a major power; in 2012 it is a regional power. This fact in 2000 presented vague "potential challenges." In 2012 China's power has potential influence on the economy and security. What is not clear is how do these generalizations justify a U.S. response? China is a rising power, but it is not an existential threat to the survival of the United States. By the

---

[1] William J. Clinton, *2001 National Security Strategy-A National Security Strategy for a Global Age*, (Washington, DC: Government Printing Office, December 2000), 64.

[2] Obama, *Sustaining U.S. Global Leadership*, 3.

United States' own admission and theirs, its co-existence with China is what fuels American economic prosperity.

It is true that China poses a more credible military capability than many other nations in the world, but that should not be the litmus test for adversaries. Moreover, the objectives are not clearly listed for the pivot to the Pacific. Is it to counter possible Chinese aggression to the United States? Is it to maintain stability in case China decides to exert aggression on other regional countries? Is it to contain China from a continued rise in the world? None of these objectives are clearly spelled out. Yet all of the proposed actions appear to take on an intent to counter balance China, save maintaining the peace on the Korean peninsula. There is no clear indication how China as a regional power and military power can affect the U.S. economy and security. Without a clear assessment there can be no strategic rationale to support the defined strategic ends. The lack of clarity regarding the 2012 update does not justify a change in strategy and engagement since the Clinton administration's 2000 statement.

COMPONENTS OF THE PIVOT

As part of the pivot, there are force structure changes and shifts. Figure 1 depicts the initial shift of forces identified by the Defense Department in the coming years to support this new policy. So without a clearly defined purpose for a pivot to the Asia-Pacific, the policy has no strategic foundation.

Figure 1: Selected U.S. Troop Deployments and Plans Map of the Asia-Pacific[3]

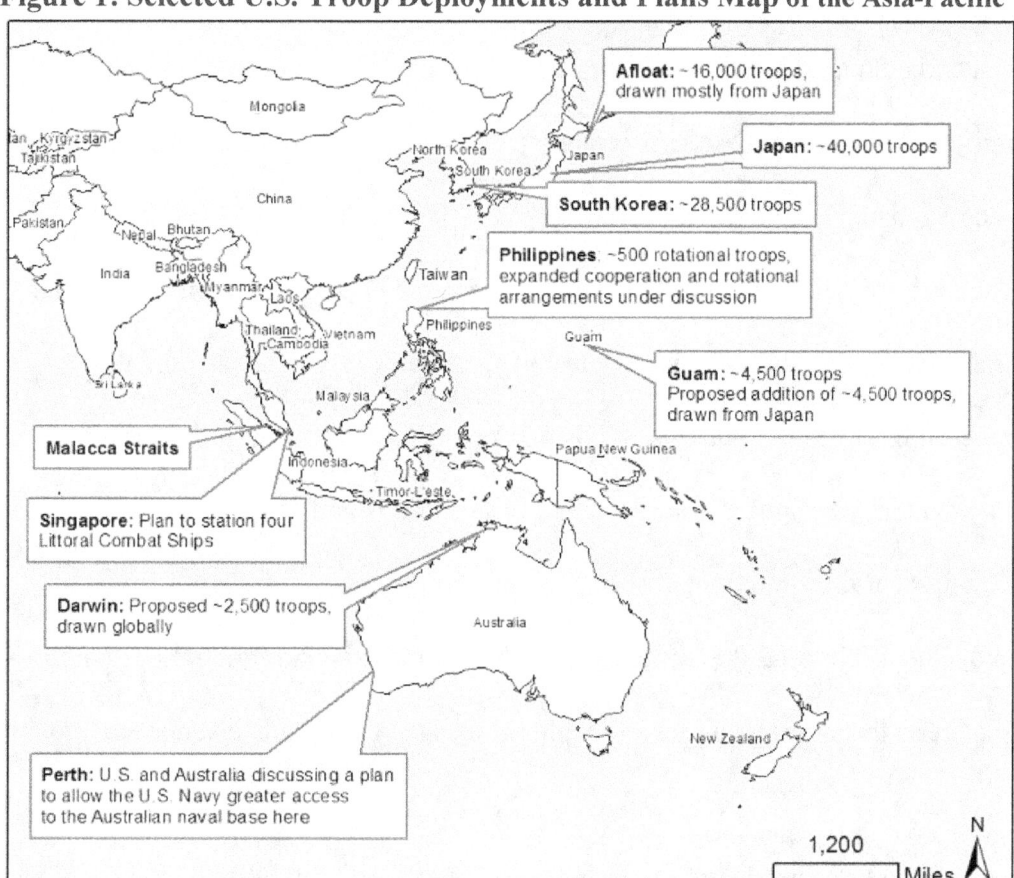

The figure above takes into account forces that have been based in Korea and Japan for decades. The force deployments to Guam, the Philippines, and Australia however are significant.

Returning to the strategic purpose of using instruments of national power to support a strategy, if there is no clear end state; military power is being deployed to serve what purpose? Examining the numbers, calls into question what those forces are there for, other than pure presence to agitate China. As an example, 2,000 Marines are proposed to be based near Darwin, Australia. The strategist should ask why they are there. The administration indicates these serve a strategic role: "Strengthened ties with

---

[3] Congressional Research Service, *Pivot to the Pacific?*, 3.

Australia, one of Washington's foremost allies, will restore a substantial American footprint near the South China Sea, a major commercial shipping route that has been increasingly the focus of Chinese territorial disputes."[4] But this is not a stated goal in the 2012 strategy update.

The territorial disputed islands of the Paracels, the Scarborough Shoals, and the Spratlys have had sovereignty claim disputes by Vietnam, China, Taiwan, and the Philippines.[5] It has been the stated U.S. position not to take sides, but it desires a peaceful resolution.[6] From this policy it is not clear those island chains even hold strategic interest for the United States. In addition, the distance from Darwin to the islands in dispute is almost 2,000 miles away. Thus, if those islands are not in stated U.S. strategic interests then there argument to deploy forces to Australia is disconnected to any strategic outcome.

Even if the U.S. decided to use these forces to address instability in those regions, the forces would have to be air or sea lifted by vessels not co-located. If the U.S. is going to have to bring in lift assets to move these forces such a great distance, one could argue, that it is more cost effective to keep them at home station and move them directly to the area. The financial cost in a time of austerity to keep this rotational or deployment force in place in Australia without a clear strategic rationale is certainly much higher.

---

[4] Matt Segal, "As Part of Pact, U.S. Marines Arrive in Australia, in China's Strategic Backyard," *New York Times*, April 4, 2012.

[5] BBC News Online, "Q&A: South China Sea Dispute," British Broadcasting Corporation, http://www.bbc.co.uk/news/world-asia-pacific-13748349 (accessed May 19, 2013).

[6] Walter Lohman, "Scarborough Shoal and Safeguarding American Interests," *Hertiage Foundation Issue Paper No. 3603* (May 14, 2012): 1. http://www.heritage.org/research/reports/2012/05/south-china-sea-dispute-between-china-and-the-philippines-safeguarding-americas-interests (accessed May 23, 2013).

Another component of the pivot is to invest as required to operate in anti-access and area denial (A2/AD) environments. The document points specifically at China when discussing the requirement to plus up these A2/AD capabilities. How are these capabilities to be used to serve U.S. strategic interests or further U.S. goals in the pacific? This is an indication of a reactive approach – not a strategy.

Increased partnering and bolstering of relationships with allies is another component of the pivot. This has been met with some skepticism regarding partners who share common interests' viability of executing this partnership building effort. The Congressional Research Service makes the following observation:

> Additionally, the prominence the Obama Administration has given to the initiative has undoubted raised the potential costs to the United States if it or successor administrations fail to follow through on public pledges. Chinese analysts have already expressed skepticism about the U.S. ability to follow through on the 'pivot,' given U.S. economic difficulties and the continuing turmoil in the Middle East, Afghanistan, and other areas. If such predictions come to pass, U.S. influence may fall further and faster due to the Obama Administrations high profile announcements.[7]

Diminished resources (a lack of means) spread to thinly across a region to support a flawed policy disguised as strategy creates conditions that will lead to a failure and unnecessary confrontation.

Recalling from Yarger's strategy theory, one can develop a strategy without current resources, but the strategy must plan to cultivate appropriate resources to meet the desired end states. Given the U.S. current and forecasted reduced defense resourcing, this drives one further in trying to understand the strategy and ask why this is critical. The U.S. defense posture is not currently planned for appropriate resourcing to engage the Asia-Pacific theater, given the extensive missions identified in the new strategy

---

[7] Congressional Research Service; *Pivot to the Pacific?*, 9-10.

document. If this is of a critical nature; the case must be clearly made and then it must be resourced or planned for resourcing in the out years. Neither of which is stated in this strategy update. It is difficult to ascertain what is really new other than hollow rhetoric. As the Congressional Research Service notes, "[a] number of the Obama Administration's discrete initiatives build on previous actions; so much so that some observers argue that the Administration has overstated the depth and extent of its pivot."[8] Arguably the United States has or will have fewer resources for defense in the coming years as compared to 2000. In effect, this leaves the U.S. in a weakened position to respond in Asia, let alone change the strategic environment.

LACK OF DESIRED ENDS and RATIONALE

The reason behind the rebalance is more about focusing on China than any other reason; thus the strategy should also lay out *why* this rebalance is so critical; it does not. From a state on state perspective or even a non-state to the United States, there is no existential threat to U.S. survival. This is where the logic of this national security strategy breaks down. What is lacking is a thorough assessment of the strategic environment and a realistic consideration of China's place in that environment.

SUMMARY

Just as the last chapter determined the 2012 national security strategy update is flawed, this pivot to Asia is flawed. There is a lack of clear reason for the pivot. The rhetoric as to why the Pacific is important to the U.S. has not changed in twenty years. The ways are not linked to the desired ends and there are minimal means to even support the laundry list of ways to use military power. What this can yield is pursuing a course of

---

[8] Ibid, 2.

action that is contains enormous uncalculated risk. While without question the Asia-Pacific theater holds many national interests, there are likely other ends to be identified, ways to support those ends with realistic means.

There is a recurring theme in many of the target areas and mission sets that a national level strategy should focus on; maintaining the domains of air, space, sea, and cyber. These are regularly referred to as the Global Commons. These Global Commons are referred to in many strategy documents (including the Defense for the 21st Century,) but are a sub tier or pillar to success.[9] A strategy that holds promise and is much more achievable is one that puts these commons at the base or foundation for U.S. grand strategy, not merely a pillar of it. The next chapter will offer insight into how to rebalance in order to preserve something that could be seen as a survival requirement for the United States – The Global Commons.

---

[9] Obama, *Sustaining U.S. Global Leadership,* 3.

CHAPTER 5: AN OPTION FOR REBALANCE-MASTERY OF THE GLOBAL COMMONS

"Global security and prosperity are increasingly dependent on the free flow of good shipped by air or sea."[1]

After thirteen years in Afghanistan and twenty-three years of national focus on Iraq, the current administration seeks to shift towards the Asia-Pacific region.[2] But as illustrated in the previous chapters, there is no strategic logic that underscores this action. The purported strategic guidance offers no rationale or structure to align to vague ends. Maintaining dominance in the Global Commons is one avenue of pragmatism without reducing influence. In fact, 2012 Strategy Update captures this well: "The United States will continue to lead global efforts with capable allies and partners to assure access to and use of the global commons, both by strengthening international norms of responsible behavior and by maintaining relevant and interoperable military capabilities."[3] Additionally, it does not put constraints to a geographical focus area nor single out single countries to presuppose aggressive actors as the pivot to Asia does in the Defense Strategic Guidance. These commons are what Barry Posen refers to as those of air, space, sea, and the cyber world.[4]

For more than 100 years, the United States has had a significant interest in the Pacific, and although the strategic environment has changed quite radically in that time –

---

[1] Obama, *Sustaining U.S. Global Leadership*, 3.

[2] While sustained combat operations of the second Iraq War began in 2003 and ended in 2010, many forces have had continuous large scale forces to counter Iraq since the build up of Desert Shield/Desert Storm in 1990. As an example there were no-fly zone (Northern Watch and Southern Watch) deployments that continued after Desert Storm all the way up to when the Operation Iraqi Freedom began.

[3] Obama, *Sustaining U.S. Global Leadership*, 3.

[4] Barry R. Posen, "Command of the Commons: The Military Foundation of U.S. Hegemony," *International Security*, 28, no. 1 (Summer 2003): 7.

American interests have remained constant: peace, security, and free trade to advance prosperity. In the post-Cold War globalized world, the global commons becomes the centerpiece of American security interests in Asia.[5] The global commons are the domains of air, space (cyberspace), and sea. It is the trade, information flow, and permissive travel to those groups who follow international order within these domains that makes them the commons. Over the past 30 years, the United States established, then dominated, the global commons.

Just as NSC-68 focused all efforts against Soviet Communism 60 years ago as the central foundation of U.S. grand strategy, the new U.S. grand strategy should focus on the global commons. While the Asia-Pacific region contains a substantial part of the commons, the network is worldwide and has significant parts in Europe, North and South America, as well as Africa. The 2010 NSS has inferences of the importance in the commons in each of the four interest areas (security, prosperity, values, and international order), but makes more overt statements in the prosperity section; however, most in-depth examination of the commons in the area of international order.[6]

Preservation and leadership in sustaining the global commons should be the baseline in *all* of the identified enduring interest areas within the strategy. Recalling that ensuring economic prosperity is the primary focus of the 2012 update this concept of the global commons should be developed further to support that enduring interest.

---

[5] Louis Morton, 'War Plan Orange: Evolution of a Strategy," *World Politics* 11, no.2 (July 1959): 221-250. This article reviews the inception and development of a War Plan against Japan to support American strategic interests starting in 1904. This article lays out the challenges the military planners faced given vague ends as well as the revisions and inter service perspectives throughout the plans development in the first four decades of the 1900s. The foundation for U.S. interests were the beginnings of what is today known as the global commons.

[6] Obama, *National Security Srategy*, 28, 49.

Figure 2 depicts the major shipping routes that represent the surface portion of the global commons. Given there is significant traffic in and around Asia, Europe still is the predominant player in trade. The inset graph shows that Asia has had substantial growth and nearly doubled its trade from 2003-2006, as did North America, while Europe, nearly doubled. The 2010 National Security Strategy is correct in assessing the strategic importance of the global commons regulated by the United States. This is good start, but it needs to be cultivated further. "The free flow of information, people, goods, and services has also advanced peace among nations, as those places have emerged more prosperous are often more stable."[7]   American enduring interests outlined in the 2010 NSS relate to this essential condition of free trade and economic prosperity, which Yarger points out are the basis for defining the strategic ends, clearly relate to the security of the global commons. This strategic assessment is correct, but the U.S. strategy should clearly identify how an effective global commons feeds all U.S. interests. Additionally, to align the ways and means the full integrated complement of U.S. national power should be focused to achieve the ends of a safe, secure, and functioning global commons – not just the military.

The following figures highlight how critical those commons are in a globalized world. From figure 2 one can determine three distinctive common sea routes. The first is the Northern Atlantic, second is through the Pacific and third is from the Pacific to the Indian Ocean and Arabian Peninsula. These predominant lanes make up the majority of sea commons for the entire world.

---

[7] Ibid, 28.

As stated earlier, the commons are more than just sea routes, air is arguably as critical as it speeds up distribution and can reach areas where shipping cannot and that are not feasible by rail or other ground transport. The following figure displays the interconnected world of globalization in the air domain through the developed routing system (figure 3).

[8] Transportcitywordpress.com, "Transitioning Skyscraper," by Justin Dillon Baatjes, Seol Han Byul, Sam Wood, http://transportcity.files.wordpress.com/2011/11/world_trade_map.jpg, (accessed February 21, 2013).

These commons are the basis for peace, security, and prosperity provides benefits for the entire world. If the United States pursued a strategy of securing the global commons it would also be supporting its enduring interests. Barry Posen points out "[c]ommand of the commons also permits the isolation of the adversary from sources of political and military support, further increasing the U.S. margin of superiority and further allowing the passage of time to work in favor of the United States."[10]

---

[9] Mapsoftheworld.com, "World Air Routes Map," http://www.mapsofworld.com/world-airroutes-map.htm. (accessed February 25, 2013).

[10] Posen, "Command of the Commons," 42.

Posen argues it is the contested zones within the commons that must be guarded against.[11] More than identifying a specific adversary or region in which domination is blatant and almost conflict provoking, a quiet U.S. dominance in the global commons will likely garner more international support if "others can be convinced that the United States is more interested in constraining regional aggressors than achieving regional dominance."[12] This assessment brings to mind the strategist's consideration of the ways to assist in achieving American security and prosperity through the global commons. Furthermore, the global commons offers a baseline for a grand strategy of overarching dominance, but not primacy. A security strategy of global commons dominance does not give a world perception of constant saber rattling which the 2012 update with its focus on China may indicate. In a time of fiscal austerity, such a strategy is logical and prudent to see the United States through the years of fiscal restraint, while still maintaining an overwhelming advantage within all domains of the global commons.

Returning to Yarger, ends are framed by "the nature of the strategic environment, and the capabilities and limitations of the instruments of power available."[13] So a potential, feasible end state is one where the United States is the leader, ensuring a stable and secure global commons. Using strategy theory, this end state is connected to and derived from a U.S. enduring interest of economic prosperity free trade, and regional security. As stated previously; from this approach the commons are a pillar of current U.S. strategy, but they are not the considered the foundation. The U.S. should harness the above and it should be the foundation of national security for the next twenty years

---

[11] Ibid, 42, passim.

[12] Posen, "Command of the Commons, 44.

[13] Yarger, 52.

and beyond. As a litmus test, examining how a secure commons matches up against Yarger's principles of strategy is worth review.

Political purpose dominates all strategy

The U.S. political purpose must be tied back to the enduring interests of America. It should not serve a specific short term administration agenda, but rather support the political purpose of the U.S. survival. From this fundamental perspective, a strategy built on maintaining the global commons will meet this principle as it supports all enduring interests.

Strategy is proactive and anticipatory

A stable and secure global commons will assist in shaping the strategic environment, while maintaining U.S. influence throughout the world. By seeking out ways to expand and secure the commons will set conditions to minimize or more effectively diffuse crisis versus merely designing a strategy to purely react to adversaries and the strategic environment. By taking a leadership role in this sustainment of the commons the U.S. will have the ability to manipulate the strategic environment and its actors worldwide.

Strategy is grounded in *what* is to be accomplished and *why* it is to be accomplished

By developing a strategy around the global commons, it will provide a clear focus as to what the nation's instruments of power actions are aimed at achieving – a stable, secure commons to bolster national security and prosperity.   It should be on the forefront of every policy decision of how this supports the commons and why a notional policy decision's implementation is required to achieve stable and secure commons.

Strategy is subordinate to the nature of the strategic environment

The global commons emerged as result of the changing strategic environment. The advancements of technology, commerce, and the majority of nations desire to increase prosperity created the conditions within the environment to pursue a global commons. As long as the strategic environment still requires powers to operate in a globalized manner then this strategy supports operating within that environment. If the strategic environment changes radically, then understandably a strategy based on a stable and secure commons might change.

Just as NSC-68 worked well within Yarger's principles of strategy, an approach founded in the global commons also meets these principles. Given the approach is sound, then determining the appropriate balance and implementation of the instruments of power must be addressed. Thus, the ways are next in the strategic equation. The commons should be secured by all aspects of the instruments of power not just the military, and not just the U.S. military. In respect to the Asia-Pacific theater, a shift in diplomatic engagement is required. The United States set conditions for many nations to prosper over the last 60 years. In many cases however the U.S. diplomacy was what Blumenthal referred to as one of "hub and spoke."[14] The U.S. current practice with alliances in the Pacific region is purely bilateral. The U.S. has five treaty based allies; Japan, South Korea, Thailand, Australia, and the Philippines.[15] The Asia-Pacific theater now has a

---

[14] Dan Blumenthal et al., "Asian Alliances in the 21st Century", Project 2049 Institute, August 30, 2011, 9. http://project2049.net/publications.html#paper (accessed March 16, 2013). The term hub and spoke refers to the United States as the hub and allied nations as the spokes.

[15] Congressional Research Service, *U.S. Strategic and Defense Relationships in the Asia-Pacific Region Report To Congress, 22 January 2007* (Washington, DC: Government Printing Office, 2007), 51. The report states "America's Asian regional alliances are based on the following treaties: The Treaty ofPeace with Japan signed in San Francisco on September 8, 1951; Security Treaty Between Australia, New Zealand and the United States (ANZUS), September 1, 1951; Mutual Defense Treaty Between the United States and the Republic of the Philippines, August 30, 1951; Mutual Defense Treaty Between the United States and the Republic of Korea, October 1, 1953; [Thailand] Southeast Asia Collective Defense Treaty (Manila Pact), September 8,1954."

great many of developed nations and requires a more integrated approach by fostering multilateral agreements; starting with current allies, and building to partner nations. Blumenthal also supports this assessment; as it is time "the alliances need to be tied into a collective network that allows them to act quickly and effectively alone and together, with or without the United States."[16] Additionally, the United States does not have to be the lead in these partnerships, but rather one who fosters the engagements. It is in these countries' best interest to help strengthen each other, versus a reliance on the United States for every strategic response in the region.

The authors of *Asian Alliances in the 21st Century* point out "primacy is the least bad option."[17] However, the above does not need to be an all or nothing approach. The United States should allow for other great powers in the region such as Japan, South Korea, and Australia to increase their presence and influence in the region, along with others such as India, the Philippines and an emerging Vietnam.

Additionally, the diplomatic and informational message would need to be refocused on this commons preservation theme. This could prove powerful in U.S. leverage with non-standard partners such as China and Russia. Global prosperity is as at risk if the commons are compromised. From strictly an Asia-Pacific perspective, current allies would need to understand this shift as U.S. strategists and policy makers truly determine what the interests are for the survival and prosperity of America and security of allies and economic partners.

One must also remember the commons are more than just in the Asia-Pacific, they are *global*. The U.S. is comfortable with allowing other nations in Europe help with

---

[16] Blumenthal et al., "Asian Alliances in the 21st Century," 10.

[17] Ibid, 2.

international order, rule of law and prosperity. It should work a strategy that bolsters

such actions globally. Understanding that Europe has NATO as the defense backbone to

assist in these matters, this author does not argue a "PATO" is advised nor required, but

the reality is these Pacific countries must be encouraged to build on the use commons

with their own means versus one dominated by the U.S. military. While focusing on the

commons, the United States can let other states balance China based on their own

relevant security interests. "[T]he country is surrounded by powerful states that could

and would check its expansion, including India and Russia, both of which have nuclear

weapons. Japan...is rich and technologically advanced enough to contribute to a

coalition of states that could balance against China."[18] With the United States leading the

protection of the commons, other countries can operate as partners in maintaining access,

or act independently without needing a U.S. security guarantee. Japan for example not

only would need to increase defense spending, but would also require amending its post-

World War II constitution to develop beyond a basic defense force.

This strategy does not come without risks. U.S. current Asia-Pacific allies

(Australia, Japan, South Korea, Thailand, and Philippines) might not agree with a global

commons focused strategy and could impact relations with those countries. These

countries could perceive that the U.S. is abandoning them or opting out of previous

established confidence that the U.S. will be the backstop for these countries' security. As

Blumenthal states; "allies may question Washington's security commitments and start to

---

[18] Barry R. Posen, "Pull Back – The Case for a Less Activist Foreign Policy," *Foreign Affairs*, January/February 2013: 123.

change their policies, either to accommodate or to challenge Beijing with more muscular military strategies of their won – perhaps including nuclear weapons."[19]

Additionally, China or other technology advanced actors could attempt to compromise the commons for gain. If the U.S. strategy seeks other major or regional powers to take on a more involved role in commons security, there is a potential for misaligned interests or power struggles could lead to an unexpected conflict. This strategy will likely put unprecedented trust with other nations.

If the United States does not move forward with a new security strategy rooted in mainly a commons access approach it will risk peril at a quickening rate. By continuing along the current strategy as Barry Posen notes "has done untold harm to U.S. national security. It makes enemies almost as fast as it slays them, discourages allies from paying for their own defense and convinces powerful states to band together and oppose Washington's plans further rising the costs of carrying out its foreign policy."[20] Moving beyond a hub and spoke of keeping a balance of power within the Asia-Pacific region is essential as the United States develops a true strategy and foreign policy in Asia.

If the U.S. takes on a central focus on the global commons there are state and non-state actors that would not fall traditionally into this specific focus. North Korea and Iran are two rogue states which are threats that do not necessarily have a strong impact on security of the commons. Dealing with those countries may require a need for a special case approach, yet U.S. grand strategy should remain unchanged. However, if in defining the problem of potential employment of weapons of mass destruction (nuclear or other) with rogue actors, then they still could fit under the grand strategy of maintaining the

---

[19] Blumenthal et al., *Asian Alliances in the 21st Century*, 5.

[20] Posen, "Pull Back", 117.

commons. "Strategic decision makers must consider not only the local consequences of a successful nuclear or biological attack on a large metropolitan area, but also the effect that such an attack would have on the global economy."[21]

---

[21] Johnathan P. Wilcox, "Legitimacy in the Conduct of Military Operations", *Short of General War: Perspectives on the Use of Military Power in the 21st Century*, (Carlisle, PA: U.S. Army War College: Strategic Studies Institute Publications, April, 2010), 11.

CONCLUSION

The question of the United States future will rely heavily on the development and adherence to a logical, feasible grand strategy or national security strategy. Currently the U.S. is blind as to what strategy should look like. The 2012 "Sustaining U.S. Global Leadership: Priorities for 21st Century Defense" document has muddied the waters both in its strategic approach as well as in what the document is supposed to represent.

Harry Yarger provides the construct for developing strategy. It is one that takes into account the strategic environment, and then uses ends, ways, and means to execute the strategy. Once the ends are determined, appropriate ways should be apportioned to meet the ends. These ways in grand strategy are segmented into four parts; diplomatic, informational, military, and economic. Within these ways are the resources or means to achieve the desired ends for the strategy. There are several axioms, which Yarger lays out in his fifteen principles to good strategy. It is important to keep these axioms in mind when developing strategy. There are several theorists that provide strategic models that could be used when examining a strategy. To keep this paper scoped this author uses Yarger to offer a logical and understandable model to examine the current national security strategy.

The U.S. has developed grand strategy in the past; most notably with the enactment of the recommendations from NSC-68. It identified the desired ends and how those would have to be achieved given the strategic environment. The ways to achieve that grand strategy identified all portions of the diplomatic, informational, military and economic spectrum. The strategy was resourced thus providing the means and finally took close eye on risk through each portion of the strategy. The review of NSC-68 provided an example of good grand strategy and set a bench mark for future national security strategies to achieve. The 2012 update to the U.S. national security strategy could be compared against both in a theoretical aspect but also in a real world example.

The most noteworthy change to national security in this document is the rebalance to the Asia-Pacific. This shift has also been referred to as the "Pivot to the Pacific" in many presidential addresses and articles as well as the common nomenclature for the U.S. State Department. While it is understandable the United States has strategic interests in this region, there seems to be a misalignment of ends, the ways to meet the ends, and the means to achieve what is desired. It arguably paints China as the next potential adversary with the only real existential threat being the impact to the U.S. economy. While China has risen over the last twenty years to be a regional power, there is no indication that China plans to threaten the sovereignty or survival of the United States.

Notwithstanding the current economic relationship which itself is a deterrent, the U.S. current strategic military options give any nation great pause to ever think of challenging the United States' sovereignty. In fact many believe, including remarks in the updated strategy that because the nations are so tightly reliant on each other the reality of the two countries going to war with each other is highly unrealistic as it is not in either one's interest. Yet the ways and means explored in the strategy update look to potentially upset the symbiotic relationship of the two nations, which could result in devastating conflict. The U.S. must be very careful in its military instrument of power in dealing with foreign policy in this region. The size and scope of the entire region already poses a risk to spreading forces too thin to accomplish any tasks set out in the guidance.

BIBLIOGRAPHY

Bartlett, Harry C., G. Paul Holman Jr., and Timothy E. Somes. "The Art of Strategy and Force Planning." In *Strategy and Force Planning*, 4th ed. Newport, RI: Naval War College Press, 2004.

Biddle, Stephen. "Strategy in War." *PS: Political Science & Politics* 3 (July 2007): 461-466.

Blumenthal, Dan, Randall Schriver, Mark Stokes, L.Cl Russell Hsiao, and Michael Mazza. "Asian Alliances in the 21st Century," (2011). http://project2049.net/publications.html#paper (accessed March 16, 2013).

Brands, Hal. *The Promise and Pitfalls of Grand Strategy*. Carlisle, PA: U.S. Army War College: Strategic Studies Institute Publications, 2012.

BBC News Online, "Q&A: South China Sea Dispute," British Broadcasting Corporation, http://www.bbc.co.uk/news/world-asia-pacific-13748349 (accessed May 19, 2013).

Clinton, William J. *2001 National Security Strategy-A National Security Strategy for a Global Age*. Washington, DC; White House, 2000.

Congressional Research Service. *National Security Strategy: Legislative Mandates, Execution to Date, and Considerations for Congress, by the Congressional Research Service, May 28, 2008*. Washington, DC: Government Printing Office, 2008.

————. *Pivot to the Pacific? The Obama Administration's 'Rebalancing' Toward Asia, by the Congressional Research Service, March 28, 2012*. Washington, DC: Government Printing Office, 2012.

Crenshaw, Martha. *Terrorism, Strategies and Grand Strategies, Attacking Terrorism*. Georgetown: Georgetown University Press, 2004.

Galula, David. *Counterinsurgency Warfare Theory and Practice*. London: Praeger Publishers, 1964.

Gray, Colin S. "RMAs and the Dimensions of Strategy," *Joint Forces Quarterly,* (Autumn/Winter 1997-98): 50-54.

Howard, Michael. "Grand Strategy in the Twentieth Century," *Defence Studies* 1, no. 1 (Spring 2001): 1-10.

Lohman, Walter, "Scarborough Shoal and Safeguarding American Interests", *Heritage Foundation Issue Paper No. 3603* (May 14, 2012):

http://www.heritage.org/research/reports/2012/05/south-china-sea-dispute-between-china-and-the-philippines-safeguarding-americas-interests (accessed May 23, 2013).

Morton, Louis. 'War Plan Orange: Evolution of a Strategy," *World Politics* 11, no. 2 (January 1959): 221-250.

Murray, Williamson and Mark Grimsley. *The Making of Strategy, Rulers, States and War.* Cambridge, UK: Cambridge University Press, 1994.

Obama, Barack. *National Security Strategy.* Washington, DC: Government Printing Office, May 2010.

Obama, Barack. *Sustaining U.S. Global Leadership: Priorities for the 21st Century Defense.* Washington DC: Government Printing Office, January 2012.

Office of the Executive Secretary to the President. *A Report to the National Security Council - NSC 68.* April 14, 1950. http://www.trumanlibrary.org/whistlestop/study_collections/coldwar/documents/pdf/10-1.pdf (accessed February 22, 2013)

Panetta, Leon. Remarks, Georgetown University, Georgetown, Washington D.C. February 6, 2013. http://www.defense.gov/Transcripts/Transcript.aspx?TranscriptID=5189 accessed February 22, 2013.

Posen, Barry R. "Command of the Commons: The Military Foundation of U.S. Hegemony," *International Security* 28, no. 1 (2003): 5-46.

———. "Pull Back – The Case for a Less Activist Foreign Policy," *Foreign Affairs*, (January/February 2013): 116-128.

Segal, Matt. "As Part of Pact, U.S. Marines Arrive in Australia, in China's Strategic Backyard.*" The New York Times*, April 4, 2012.

Wilcox, Johnathan P. "Legitimacy in the Conduct of Military Operations," in *Short of General War: Perspectives on the Use of Military Power in the 21st Century*, edited by Harry R. Yarger. Carlisle, PA: U.S. Army War College: Strategic Studies Institute Publications, April, 2010.

Yarger, Harry R., *The Little Book on Big Strategy,* Carlisle, PA: U.S. Army War College: Strategic Studies Institute Publications, 2006.

Zakaria, Fareed. "Stop searching for an Obama Doctrine," *The New York Times*, July 6, 2011.